Cats

Julie Murray

abdopublishing.com

Published by Abdo Kids, a division of ABDO, PO Box 398166, Minneapolis, Minnesota 55439.
Copyright © 2016 by Abdo Consulting Group, Inc. International copyrights reserved in all countries.
No part of this book may be reproduced in any form without written permission from the publisher.

Printed in the United States of America, North Mankato, Minnesota.

052015

092015

THIS BOOK CONTAINS
RECYCLED MATERIALS

Photo Credits: iStock, Shutterstock

Production Contributors: Teddy Borth, Jennie Forsberg, Grace Hansen

Design Contributors: Candice Keimig, Dorothy Toth

Library of Congress Control Number: 2014958422

Cataloging-in-Publication Data

Murray, Julie.
 Cats / Julie Murray.
  p. cm. -- (Family pets)
ISBN 978-1-62970-899-7
Includes index.
1. Cats--Juvenile literature. 2. Pets--Juvenile literature.   I. Title.
636.8--dc23
                    2014958422

Table of Contents

Cats

Cats make great family pets.

Cats have soft fur.

They like to be pet.

Cats have **whiskers**.

These help them feel.

Cats have **claws**.

They like to scratch things.

Cats need food and water.

Noah feeds his cat.

12

Cats need a litter box.

It has to be kept clean.

Cats need brushing.

Lila brushes her cat.

Cats should see a **veterinarian**.

This keeps them healthy.

Is a cat the right pet for your family?

Cat Supplies

cat food

litter box

cat toy

scratching post

Glossary

claws
curved, sharp nails on
some animals.

whiskers
long hairs that grow from the
faces of many animals.

veterinarian
a person who went to school
to treat hurt or sick animals.

Index

abdokids.com

Use this code to log on to abdokids.com and access crafts, games, videos, and more!

Abdo Kids Code:
FAK8997